Lexile: _860 L_

AR/BL: _5.3_

AR Points: _0.5_

EXPERIMENTS WITH MAGIC

A TRUE BOOK®

by
Salvatore Tocci

Children's Press®
A Division of Scholastic Inc.

New York Toronto London Auckland Sydney
Mexico City New Delhi Hong Kong
Danbury, Connecticut

These are water molecules. You can use the solid, liquid, and gas forms of water to do magic tricks.

Reading Consultant
Susan Virgilio

Science Consultant
Tenley Andrews

The photo on the cover shows magic props. The photo on the title page shows a magician pulling a rabbit out of his hat.

The author and publisher are not responsible for injuries or accidents that occur during or from any experiments. Experiments should be conducted in the presence of or with the help of an adult. Any instructions of the experiments that require the use of sharp, hot, or other unsafe items should be conducted by or with the help of an adult.

Library of Congress Cataloging-in-Publication Data

Tocci, Salvatore.
    Experiments with magic / by Salvatore Tocci.
        p. cm. (A True book)
    Includes bibliographical references and index.
    Contents: Have you ever done a magic trick? — What can you do with water? — Experiment 1, Flowing upward — Experiment 2, Pouring out — Experiment 3, Staying in — What can you do with air? — Experiment 4, Dropping in — Experiment 5, Firing away — Experiment 6, Floating in air — What can you do with light? — Experiment 7, Spinning around — Experiment 8, Looking upside down — Fun with magic — Experiment 9, Turning colors.
    ISBN 0-516-22788-2 (lib. bdg.)   0-516-27808-8 (pbk.)
    1. Science—Experiments—Juvenile literature. 2. Magic— Experiments—Juvenile literature. [1. Science—Experiments. 2. Magic— Experiments. 3. Experiments.] I. Title. II. Series.
Q164 .T674 2003
507.8—dc21
                                                                2002015259

CHILDREN'S PRESS, and A TRUE BOOK®, and associated logos are trademarks and or registered trademarks of Scholastic Library Publishing.
SCHOLASTIC and associated logos are trademarks and or registered trademarks of Scholastic Inc.
1 2 3 4 5 6 7 8 9 10 R 12 11 10 09 08 07 06 05 04 03

Contents

Have You Ever Done a Magic Trick?

Have you ever seen a magician perform in person or on television? Many people consider Harry Houdini to be the greatest magician who ever performed. Houdini lived from 1874 to 1926. During his lifetime, he amazed people all over the world with his feats of magic.

Houdini once made a 10,000-pound (4,540-kilogram) elephant disappear on a stage in a New York City theater, in front of a live audience. In 1913, he performed what most people think was his greatest escape trick. It was called the "Upside-Down Water Torture Cell." For this trick, Houdini had his feet locked in an iron brace. He was then lowered headfirst into a tank full of water. An iron gate was then locked into place on top of the tank. Finally, a curtain was placed over the tank. People waited anxiously to see what happened to Houdini. To everyone's amazement, Houdini always managed to escape and walk out dripping wet from underneath the curtain.

Houdini performed complicated and dangerous tricks that took years of practice to perfect. However, you can perform some simple magic tricks to amaze your family and friends by doing the experiments in this book.

You will also learn the secrets behind these tricks. As you will discover, these secrets are really scientific explanations. Magicians never reveal their secrets. However, you should reveal the scientific explanations to your audience after you have performed your magic tricks.

What Can You Do With Water?

Water is a very unusual substance. For example, water is one of the very few things that you can find as a solid, liquid, and gas all at the same time and in the same place, such as your kitchen. You can find it as a solid (ice)

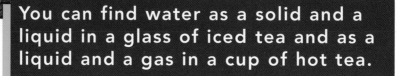

You can find water as a solid and a liquid in a glass of iced tea and as a liquid and a gas in a cup of hot tea.

in the freezer, as a liquid (water) from a faucet, and as a gas (steam) from water boiling in a pot. Learn how you can use water to perform some magic tricks.

Flowing Upward

You will need:
- two empty 2-liter plastic soda bottles
- food coloring
- shallow pan
- piece of aluminum foil

Fill one bottle with cold water. Fill the other bottle with hot water. Make sure both bottles are filled to the very top. Tell your audience that you will make colored water magically rise to the top of one of the bottles.

Add food coloring to the hot water until it has a dark color and place the bottle in the pan. Cover the top of the bottle filled with cold water with the aluminum foil. While holding the foil over the mouth, carefully turn the bottle of cold water upside down and set it on top of the bottle filled with hot water.

Use one hand to hold the bottles in place. Use your other hand to pull the foil out from between the bottles. Your audience will be surprised to see the colored water flow upward into the clear water on top.

Hot water, like hot air, rises. As a result, the colored water from the bottom bottle rises.

The hot water in the bottom bottle flows upward, while the cold water in the top bottle flows downward. Hot water has a lower **density** than does cold water. Density refers to how much **matter**, or stuff, is in a given space. For example, think of your classroom as the given space. Now imagine that there are ten students in the room. The density of the room can be written as "ten students/classroom." Then imagine that ten more students enter the room. Now the density is twenty students/classroom. With more students in the same space, the room now has a higher density.

Because hot water has a lower density than cold water, it rises from the bottom bottle and flows into the top bottle filled with cold water.

Can you explain why the box with six marbles has twice the density as the box with three marbles?

As the hot water rises, the food coloring also rises.

Because cold water has a higher density than hot water, cold water in the top bottle moves downward and flows into the bottom bottle filled with hot water.

Challenge your audience to do the same trick, but fill both bottles with cold water. This time, the food coloring will stay in the bottom bottle. Now learn how you can perform a trick in which you change the way water flows with a snap of your fingers.

Experiment 2

Pouring Out

Ask an adult to help you use the hammer and nail to punch four tiny holes near the bottom of the can. The holes must be no more than 1/4-inch (0.5 centimeter) from one another. Cover the holes with tape and fill the can with water. Tell your audience that you can magically change the way water flows.

Set the can on the table so that it sticks out past the edge. Place the bucket on the floor beneath the can. Remove the tape from the can. The water will start pouring out in four tiny streams from each hole.

Tell your audience that you will now make the water pour out as a single stream. To do this, use your thumb and index finger to "squeeze" the four streams together. Remove your hand. The water will now pour out of the can in one large stream.

Bring your thumb and finger together slowly. The water will then start pouring out of the can in a single stream.

Tell your audience that you will get the water to flow in four separate streams again. Place your thumb and index finger in the center of the larger stream and flick them outward. The water will separate into four tiny streams.

Water is made of very tiny particles called **molecules.** Another unusual thing about water is that its molecules are strongly attracted to one another. When your fingers "squeeze" the four tiny streams, the water molecules stick together to make one large stream. When you flick your fingers, you overcome this attractive force between the molecules. The water molecules are then forced apart and again flow in four tiny streams. Now show your audience how you can make water stay inside a container even though it has a hole in it.

Staying In

You will need:
- adult helper
- hammer
- thin nail
- large plastic bottle with screw-on cap
- bucket

Ask an adult to help you use the hammer and nail to punch a hole in the bottom of the bottle. Also punch a hole near the top. Show your audience the hole in the bottom of the bottle, but not the hole near the top. Tell your audience that you can magically keep a bottle from leaking even though it has a hole in the bottom.

Do not make the holes too large.

Fill the bucket with water. Submerge the bottle in the bucket so that it fills with water. Screw on the cap. Place a finger over the hole you made near the top of the bottle. Lift the bottle and show it to your audience. After a few drops fall out of the bottom hole, the bottle will stop leaking.

Ask someone in your audience to hold the bottle. Without their finger covering the hole at the top, water will start to pour out of the bottle. Take the bottle back, again covering the top hole with your finger. The bottle will stop leaking.

Water will pour out of the bottom hole as long as the top hole is not covered.

When you cover the top hole, you prevent air from entering the bottle. The air is filled with gas molecules such as oxygen and carbon dioxide. These gas molecules are always moving and pushing against things. This creates **air pressure**. Air pressure is the force of air pushing against something, such as our bodies.

The air inside a tire pushes against its wall and keeps it inflated. If the pressure is too low, more air must be pumped into the tire to increase the pressure and keep it inflated.

Air cannot enter the top hole when your finger covers it. As a result, there is not enough air pressure to push down on the water and force it out of the bottom hole. However, when you uncover the top hole, air enters and there is enough air pressure to force water out of the bottom hole. Learn some other tricks you can do with air.

What Can You Do With Air?

A **barometer** measures changes in air pressure. A falling barometer means that air pressure is dropping and that rain may be on the way. In contrast, a rising barometer means that the air pressure is rising and that nice weather is

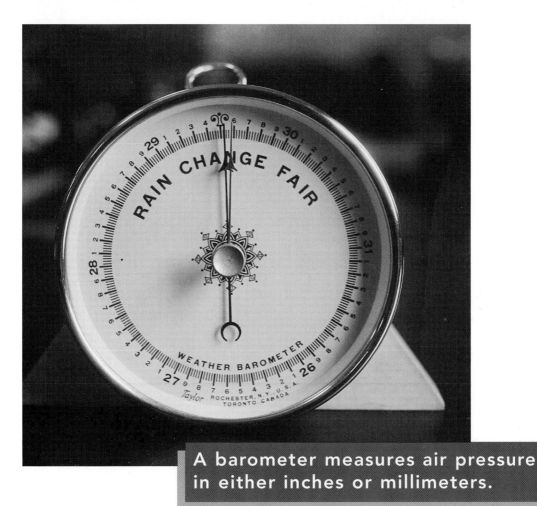

A barometer measures air pressure
in either inches or millimeters.

approaching. Learn how you
can change air pressure to
perform a magic trick.

Dropping In

You will need:
- adult helper
- small pot
- stove
- egg
- paper towel
- matches
- glass bottle or jar with a mouth large enough to let an egg nearly pass through it

Ask an adult to help you hard-boil the egg. After the egg cools, peel it. Tell your audience that you can get the egg inside the bottle without pushing or breaking it.

Have the adult light the paper towel on fire and drop it into the bottle. Set the smaller end of the egg on the mouth of the bottle. Watch what happens to the egg.

The egg will wobble a little before it drops into the bottle.

The higher air pressure outside the bottle pushes down on the egg more than the lower air pressure inside the bottle pushes up on the egg.

The heat from the burning towel warms the air inside the bottle. Like hot water, hot air also rises. The hot air rises out of the bottle, sliding past the egg. As the hot air escapes, the air pressure inside the bottle drops. The air pressure on the outside is higher, pushing the egg into the bottle. Now see how you can push on air to do another magic trick.

Firing Away

You will need:
- scissors
- empty 2-liter plastic soda bottle
- plastic wrap
- rubber band
- adult helper
- matches
- candle
- ruler

Cut the bottom off the bottle. Cover the hole with three layers of plastic wrap. Use the rubber band to hold the plastic wrap tightly against the bottle. Tell your audience that you can put out a candle flame without blowing on it and without squeezing the bottle.

Ask an adult to light the candle. Hold the bottle about 6 inches (15 cm) from the candle. Point the mouth of the bottle at the flame and tap the center of the plastic wrap with your finger.

When you tap the bottle, the plastic wrap pushes on the air inside the bottle. The air

26

is forced out of the opening at the other end of the bottle and puts out the flame. Experiment to see how far away you can hold the bottle and still put out the flame. Also see what happens when you point the bottle at other objects like a dish of water, pieces of paper, and a table tennis ball. Then use the table tennis ball to do another magic trick with air.

Experiment 6

Floating in Air

You will need:
- powerful hair dryer
- table tennis ball
- empty toilet paper tube

Point the hair dryer toward the ceiling and turn it on high. Tell your audience that you can make a table tennis ball float in the air.

Place the table tennis ball in the path of the hair dryer and watch it float in the air. With the ball floating in air, walk slowly. The ball should stay floating above the hair dryer. Next, slowly tilt the hair dryer to one side. The ball should also move toward the side. Now, slowly lower the paper tube over the ball. The ball should get sucked up into the tube.

DEATH OF THE CYCLOPES

Apollo was the god of light, music, and healing. He had a human son named Asclepius (ahs-KLEE-pee-uhss). Asclepius was a skilled **healer** like his father.

Myths say Asclepius knew how to bring the dead back to life. Zeus did not want a human to have this power. He killed Asclepius with a lightning bolt.

Apollo was angry at Zeus, but he knew he was not strong enough to harm Zeus. So, Apollo killed the three Cyclopes. They had made the lightning bolt Zeus used to kill Apollo's son.

Zeus punished Apollo for killing the Cyclopes. He made Apollo take care of King Admetus' (ad-MEE-tuhss) cattle for one year. This task embarrassed Apollo.

Later, Zeus felt sorry that he had killed Asclepius. Asclepius had performed many good deeds by healing people who were sick. Zeus brought Asclepius back to life and made him a god of healing and medicine.

Nicolas Poussin's painting *Landscape with Polyphemus* shows the Cyclops Polyphemus (top center) sitting on a mountain. He is playing a love song for Galatea (bottom center, seated on rock).

POLYPHEMUS

Myths tell about another group of Cyclopes. They lived in mountain caves on Sicily. Sicily is an island near Italy.

Some myths say the Cyclopes on Sicily were related to the first three Cyclopes. But they were not as skilled as the first three Cyclopes. The island Cyclopes were neither blacksmiths nor builders. Instead, they raised sheep and goats.

The Cyclops Polyphemus was the son of the sea god Poseidon (poh-SYE-duhn). Polyphemus was the biggest and strongest of the island Cyclopes. Myths say that he liked to sink ships and eat sailors.

One day, Telemus (TE-li-muhss) visited Sicily. Telemus was a **seer** and told people about their future. He told Polyphemus that a great hero would come to Sicily and blind him. At the time, Polyphemus did not listen to Telemus' warning. All Polyphemus thought about was a beautiful sea **nymph** named Galatea (gah-luh-TEE-uh).

Giulio Romano's painting *Polyphemus, Acis, and Galatea* shows
Acis and Galatea (bottom right) hiding from Polyphemus.

GALATEA AND ACIS

Polyphemus loved Galatea, but he worried that she thought he was an ugly monster. So, he combed his messy hair and trimmed his shaggy beard. Polyphemus even sang a love song to impress Galatea.

Galatea did not love Polyphemus. She loved a young man named Acis (UH-siss). Acis was the son of a sea nymph. As Polyphemus sang, Galatea and Acis hid together behind a rock.

After Polyphemus' song was over, Galatea and Acis thought it was safe to come out from their hiding place. But Polyphemus saw them together. He became very angry.

Galatea and Acis tried to flee from Polyphemus. Galatea dived into the ocean, but Acis did not escape. Polyphemus picked up a piece of a mountain and dropped it on Acis.

Acis' blood flowed from under the mountain. Myths say his blood slowly turned to water. Acis' blood became a river that flows from the foot of Mount Etna in Sicily.

This ancient Roman painting shows Odysseus (left) with the Cyclops Polyphemus (right).

POLYPHEMUS AND ODYSSEUS

The Greek hero Odysseus stopped on Sicily as he sailed home after a great war. He went ashore with several of his men. They needed food and fresh water.

Odysseus and his men found a large cave filled with baskets of fruits, vegetables, and cheese. They waited in the cave for the owner of the food to return.

The food belonged to Polyphemus. He led a flock of sheep into the cave. Then, Polyphemus rolled a large rock in front of the cave's entrance. Odysseus and his men were trapped inside.

Odysseus asked Polyphemus if he and his men could have some of the food. Polyphemus laughed. He grabbed two of Odysseus' men, ate them, and then went to sleep.

Odysseus knew he could not kill Polyphemus while the monster slept. Odysseus and his men would be trapped. They could not move the large rock that blocked the cave's entrance. Odysseus needed to think of a plan to escape.

Odysseus and his men are shown blinding Polyphemus on this
Greek vase. Ancient Greeks decorated everyday items like vases,
cups, and bowls with scenes from myths.

ODYSSEUS ESCAPES

In the morning, Polyphemus ate two of Odysseus' men and then led his sheep outside. Polyphemus blocked the cave's entrance with the rock while he was gone. At night, Polyphemus came back and ate two more men before going to sleep.

Odysseus and his men had sharpened a large log while Polyphemus was outside. As Polyphemus slept, they poked the Cyclops in the eye with the log. Polyphemus woke and roared in pain, but he could not see the men to catch them.

In the morning, Polyphemus moved the rock to let his sheep out. He could not see Odysseus and his men. So, Polyphemus stood in the cave's entrance to keep them from escaping. But the men tricked Polyphemus. They tied themselves to the sheep's bellies. The men escaped as the sheep walked out of the cave.

Polyphemus asked his father, Poseidon, to punish Odysseus. For 10 years, Poseidon stopped Odysseus from sailing home. Poseidon raised storms that sunk Odysseus' ships.

The Cyclopean walls around the ancient city of Mycenae, Greece, were built about 3,000 years ago. The city entrance pictured above is called the Lion's Gate.

MYTHOLOGY TODAY

Myths help people learn about ancient **cultures**. Historians are not sure why people imagined monsters with one eye. The idea may have come from ancient blacksmiths. Some experts believe blacksmiths wore an eye patch over one eye to protect it while they worked. Like these blacksmiths, Cyclopes used only one eye. Other experts believe that a group of blacksmiths had tattoos of an eye or a circle on their foreheads. Cyclopes had one eye on their foreheads similar to the blacksmiths' tattoos.

Names from ancient myths are common today. Myths say the Cyclopes made walls by stacking large rocks on top of each other. Today, walls made of large rocks are called Cyclopean walls. In Marvel Enterprises' X-men comic, Cyclops is the name of a superhero. He shoots a powerful red ray from his eyes.

People no longer believe that Greek and Roman myths are true. These myths are now told for people's enjoyment. They are exciting stories about heroes and their adventures.

GLOSSARY

ancient (AYN-shunt)—very old

culture (KUHL-chur)—a people's way of life, ideas, art, customs, and traditions

healer (HEE-lur)—a person who cures other people's illnesses; healers in myths often used potions and herbs to cure people.

nymph (NIMF)—a female spirit or goddess found in a meadow, a forest, a mountain, a sea, or a stream

Olympian (oh-LIM-pee-uhn)—one of 12 powerful gods who ruled the world from Mount Olympus

overthrow (oh-vur-THROH)—to defeat and remove a leader from power

seer (SEE-ur)—a person who can see the future

sibling (SIB-ling)—a brother or a sister

thunderbolt (THUHN-dur-bohlt)—Zeus' magic weapon; Zeus used the thunderbolt to throw lightning bolts at his enemies.

Titan (TYE-ten)—one of 12 giants who ruled the world before the Olympians

READ MORE

Fanelli, Sara. *Mythological Monsters of Ancient Greece.* Cambridge, Mass.: Candlewick Press, 2002.

Hoena, B. A. *Odysseus.* World Mythology. Mankato, Minn.: Capstone Press, 2004.

USEFUL ADDRESSES

National Junior Classical League
422 Wells Mill Drive
Miami University
Oxford, OH 45056

Ontario Classical Association
P.O. Box 19505
55 Bloor Street West
Toronto, ON M4W 1A5
Canada

INTERNET SITES

FactHound offers a safe, fun way to find Internet sites related to this book. All of the sites on FactHound have been researched by our staff.

Here's how:
1. Visit *www.facthound.com*
2. Type in this special code **0736824979** for age-appropriate sites. Or, enter a search word related to this book for a more general search.
3. Click on the **Fetch It** button.

FactHound will fetch the best sites for you!

INDEX